WHO WERE THE ACCUSED WITCHES OF SALEM?

And Other Questions about the Witchcraft Trials

Laura Hamilton Waxman

LERNER PUBLICATIONS COMPANY · MINNEAPOLIS

A Word about Language

English word usage, spelling, grammar, and punctuation have changed over the centuries. Some spellings in this book have been changed from the original for better understanding.

Lerner Publications Company
A division of Lerner Publishing Group, Inc.
241 First Avenue North
Minneapolis, MN 55401 U.S.A.

Website address: www.lernerbooks.com

Library of Congress Cataloging-in-Publication Data

Waxman, Laura Hamilton.
    Who were the accused witches of Salem? : and other questions about the
witchcraft trials / by Laura Hamilton Waxman.
        p.   cm. — (Six questions of American history)
    Includes bibliographical references and index.
    ISBN 978–0–7613–5225–9 (lib. bdg. : alk. paper)
      1. Trials (Witchcraft)—Massachusetts—Salem—History—17th century.
2. Witchcraft—Massachusetts—Salem—History—17th century. 3. Salem
(Mass.)—History—Colonial period, ca. 1600–1775. 4. Witchcraft—History.
I. Title.
KFM2478.8.W5W39 2012
133.4'3097445—dc23   2011022553

Manufactured in the United States of America
1 – DP – 12/31/11

TABLE OF CONTENTS · · · · · · · · · · · · · · **4**

THE SIX
QUESTIONS
HELP YOU
DISCOVER THE
FACTS!

INTRODUCTION

Deep in the winter of January 1692, something terrifying began happening in Massachusetts. Two girls from a community known as Salem Village came down with a strange illness. They went into fits that made their bodies shake and twist into odd positions. Sometimes they crawled on the floor and hid under tables. They complained of being pinched, bitten, and choked. At other times, they couldn't speak at all.

Their family was desperate to cure them. They brought in doctor after doctor. They prayed for the girls to get well. Nothing worked. The girls only seemed to grow sicker.

More than a month later, a local doctor gave his opinion. The girls were not sick, he said. He believed they had a much worse problem. A witch, he said, was tormenting them with invisible and evil powers. The witch might be anyone, including a friend, a neighbor, or a household member. This idea struck terror in the hearts of the villagers. That terror led to a deadly event—the Salem Witch Trials (questionings in a court of law)—that would secure Salem's place in U.S. history.

The Salem Witch Museum in Salem, Massachusetts

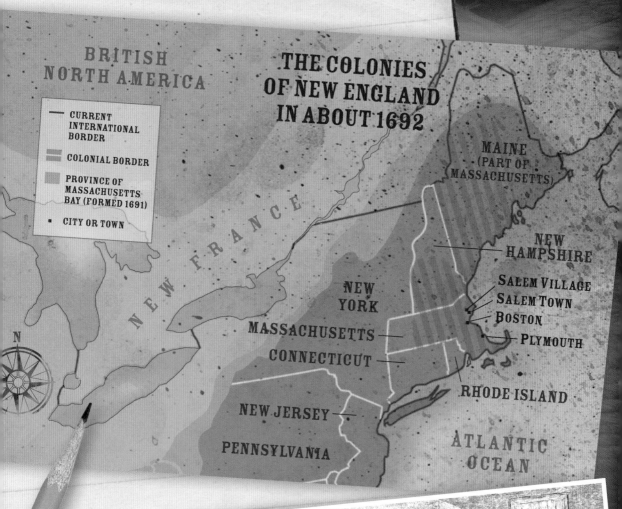

THE COLONIES
OF NEW ENGLAND
IN ABOUT 1692

BRITISH
NORTH AMERICA

Legend:
- CURRENT INTERNATIONAL BORDER
- COLONIAL BORDER
- PROVINCE OF MASSACHUSETTS BAY (FORMED 1691)
- CITY OR TOWN

NEW FRANCE

MAINE
(PART OF MASSACHUSETTS)

NEW HAMPSHIRE

NEW YORK

SALEM VILLAGE
SALEM TOWN
BOSTON

MASSACHUSETTS

PLYMOUTH

CONNECTICUT

RHODE ISLAND

NEW JERSEY

PENNSYLVANIA

ATLANTIC OCEAN

N

A woman named as a witch argues her case in front of a judge. The person who named her, a young girl, lies on the floor. This image was created in 1754.

A group of Puritan churchgoers walks through the snow in the Massachusetts Bay Colony in the 1620s.

ONE TROUBLE BREWING

Salem Village was located in the Massachusetts Bay Colony. This British territory eventually became the modern state of Massachusetts. Like all British colonists, the people of Massachusetts lived under British rule. But they enjoyed greater religious freedom than people back in England.

Many colonists living in Massachusetts were Puritans. Puritans wanted to make changes to the Church of England. The Church of England was the nation's official religion, and British people were expected

a faraway territory settled by people from a nation who agree to live under that nation's rule

a large religious group in England that wanted to make changes to the country's official religion. Puritans settled the Massachusetts Bay Colony in the 1600s.

to follow it strictly. Puritans disagreed with many of the church's beliefs and practices. Because of their outspokenness, Puritans were often mistreated. Thousands of them fled to New England in the 1600s.

Puritans believed good Christians should give up fancy clothing and grand homes. They should work hard and pray often. They should avoid having much free time. That way they wouldn't be tempted to stray from their strict beliefs and values.

In Massachusetts they set up tight-knit Puritan communities. Salem Town was one of the oldest of these communities. The thriving seaport had become a bustling city. In the Bay Colony, only Boston was bigger.

Smaller farming communities lay beyond Salem Town. The closest was Salem Village. It had about 200 adults and perhaps 550 people in all. The village was officially part of Salem Town. It had the reputation of being a quarrelsome community. The villagers always seemed to be arguing about one thing or another.

SALEM VILLAGE
Salem Village was later renamed Danvers. Salem Town became modern-day Salem, Massachusetts, not far from Danvers.

old site of
Salem Village

95

Wenham

Danvers

114

Beverly

107

128

Salem

old site of Salem Town

MASSACHUSETTS

GPS

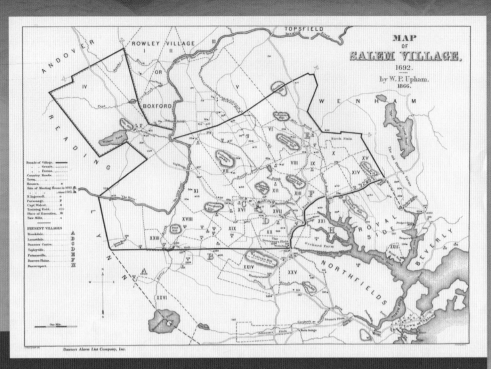

This map shows the boundaries of Salem Village, Massachusetts, in 1692. Salem Town is located on the coast by the South River (lower right).

One of the biggest disagreements involved the community's future. Some villagers wanted Salem Village to separate from Salem Town. That way it could have its own town government and make its own choices. But other villagers disagreed. They thought the village was better off the way it was, and they fought against any changes. This disagreement caused a lot of anger in the community. At times it seemed to turn the villagers against one another.

Another problem involved the village's minister. The minister held great importance in the community. But the villagers could never agree on who had the power to choose the minister. As a result, some villagers were always unhappy with the decision.

HOW DID ARGUMENTS GROW BETWEEN THE VILLAGERS?

Like other communities, Salem had its share of disagreements. One villager might accuse another of stealing his cow. Or two neighbors might disagree over the boundaries of their property. But because it was officially part of Salem Town, Salem Village did not have a local government to settle those disagreements. As a result, arguments between villagers often dragged on and on. Over time enemies formed and tensions grew. This encouraged people to later turn against one another during the Salem Witch Trials.

In 1689 a new minister got drawn into this ongoing argument. His name was Samuel Parris. Instead of working for peace in the community, Parris seemed to make matters worse. In his church sermons, or speeches, Parris spoke often of the devil. Like many Christians, Puritans believed that the devil was God's greatest enemy. The devil's goal was to turn people away from the Puritan way of life.

This 1685 painting of Samuel Parris was pasted inside a locket.

Parris claimed that the devil and certain wicked people in the community were against him. They wanted to destroy the church, he said. To the villagers, Parris seemed to be judging anyone who disliked him. He seemed to be saying that those who disagreed with him were bad people. His words added to the feelings of resentment, fear, and uncertainty in the community.

Those feelings only grew with the start of a war in New York, New Hampshire, and Maine. Later known as King William's War (1689–1697), the fighting took place between British colonists and their Native American neighbors.

This colored woodcut from 1850 shows a raid by American Indian and French attackers on the settlers of Schenectady, New York. The raid, which took place in February 1690, was part of King William's War.

The Native Americans hoped to force British colonists off what had been their land.

The people of Salem feared that the bloody fighting would soon reach Massachusetts. Like most Puritans, they did not understand or respect their American Indian neighbors. They believed Native Americans were somehow connected to the devil. This belief created an intense fear of native people. The added worry of being attacked only strengthened that fear.

All of these problems made Salem Village a tense and troubled place. The community was like a pile of wood that could be set to flames with a single match. In 1692 the fear of witches became that match. It lit up the village with terror. And that terror spread like wildfire.

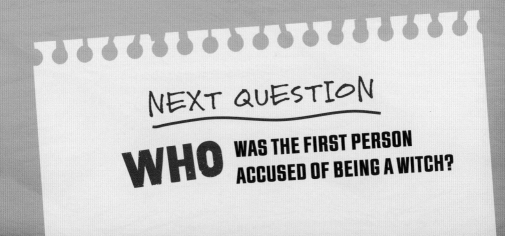

NEXT QUESTION

WHO WAS THE FIRST PERSON ACCUSED OF BEING A WITCH?

In 1891 the *New England Magazine* showed this sketch of the home where Samuel Parris and his family lived.

TWO SALEM BEWITCHED

The trouble began with the two girls who fell ill in the bitterly cold January of 1692. One of them was Samuel Parris's daughter Elizabeth, or Betty. The other was his niece Abigail Williams. Both of them lived with Parris and his wife, Elizabeth.

Rumor traveled fast in the village. By late February, everyone had heard that the girls were thought to be bewitched. This news shocked the community. Like most Puritans, the people of Salem Village believed in witches. They thought witches were people who worked for the devil. Usually witches were women, but they could also be men.

bewitched. under the power of a witch

12

Back then, many people believed witches had the power to practice a harmful magic known as witchcraft. Using witchcraft, they could sicken a farmer's cow or spoil butter. They could cause a terrible storm or make a baby ill. They could even cause someone's death. A look, a touch, or a word from a witch had the power to cause great harm. Most disturbing, Puritans thought a witch could be in two places at once. Her body might be in one place while her ghostlike spirit traveled somewhere else.

Joseph E. Baker (1837–1914) painted this courtroom scene showing a woman named as a witch causing lightning strikes and other evil magic.

Back in England, a person who practiced harmful witchcraft was put to death. Massachusetts followed the same law. Even so, few people in the colony had been killed for practicing witchcraft. Usually it was too difficult to prove that a person was a witch.

At first, neither Abigail nor Betty accused anyone of harming them. They didn't blame anyone for their suffering.

accused | claimed that someone has committed a crime

Ministers from other towns told Parris to pray and wait. They believed God would heal the girls in time.

Not everyone in the community agreed. Better to find the witch and punish her, they said. Otherwise, she might harm others. Even worse, the witch might tempt someone to join her in working for the devil.

In late February, a friend of the Parrises decided to take action. She asked the family's two slaves to bake something called a witch cake. The slaves, named Tituba and John, worked for Samuel Parris without pay. The Parrises' friend told the slaves to feed witch cake to the family dog. This ritual was

WHAT STORIES WERE TOLD ABOUT THE BEWITCHED GIRLS?

Legend has it that Betty and Abigail took part in some magic before they fell ill. One story says that Tituba showed them an old-fashioned way of telling their fortunes. Another story says that a larger group of village girls came together to practice doing magic. The magic wasn't real, but the girls believed it was. According to the legend, the experience frightened them and caused them to think they were bewitched. Most modern historians no longer believe those stories are accurate.

supposed to bring the witch out of hiding.

The ritual didn't work. Instead, the girls grew sicker than ever. By the next day, they started to accuse Tituba of being a witch. As a slave, Tituba had no power in the community. Her dark skin and non-Christian background made her an outsider.

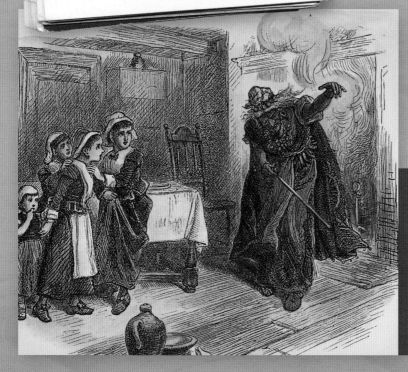

This print from 1878 shows Tituba performing acts of witchcraft for Betty and Abigail. The image appeared in *A Popular History of the United States*, volume 2, by William Cullen Bryant.

Meanwhile, two other village girls fell ill. They were Ann Putnam and Elizabeth (Betty) Hubbard. Right away Ann and Betty started accusing witches of harming them. They named two new people, Sarah Good and Sarah Osborne. The girls said that these women's spirits had entered their homes. They said the women had used witchcraft to secretly torture them day and night.

Like Tituba, Good and Osborne were outsiders in the community. Sarah Good and her family were homeless. She begged other villagers for food or a place to stay. Often she seemed nasty or ungrateful to those who helped her. Her unpleasant personality made her very unpopular. She fit people's image of a bitter and cruel witch.

Sarah Osborne was old and frail, and she hadn't been to church in months. Years ago she had married one of her younger male servants. The community frowned on this marriage.

Another illustration by Pyle shows the residents of Salem suspiciously eyeing an old woman with a black cat at the time of the witch crisis.

In addition, she was at odds with Ann Putnam's family. The Putnams believed Osborne had taken some of their land.

Ann Putnam's family decided to take action. On February 29, three of Ann's relatives walked to Salem Town. There they demanded that the town's leaders arrest Tituba, Good, and Osborne.

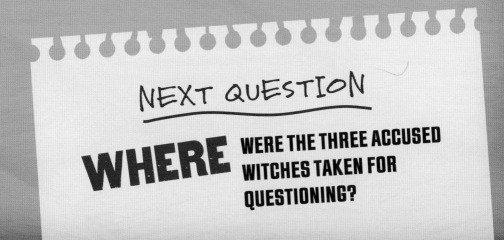

NEXT QUESTION

WHERE WERE THE THREE ACCUSED WITCHES TAKEN FOR QUESTIONING?

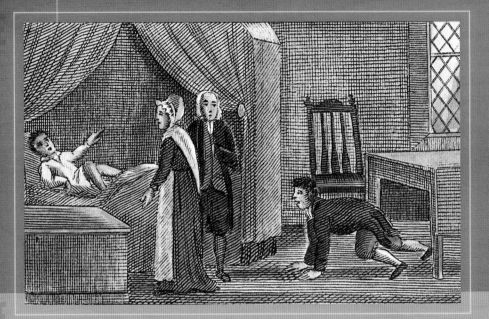

In this wood engraving (print) from around 1830, children appear struck with illness and insanity as a result of witchcraft in Salem.

THREE QUESTIONING THE ACCUSED

The next morning, two men came to Salem Village. John Hathorne and Jonathan Corwin were leaders from Salem Town. Their job was to question the three women. They also planned to question the four bewitched girls and other community members. Their questions would help uncover evidence against the women. If the men found enough evidence, the women would later be put on trial. A trial would allow a court of law to make an official decision about each of the accused.

information that is considered proof in a court of law

In past witchcraft cases, accused witches were usually questioned in private. But Hathorne and Corwin chose to question the three women in front of the entire community. They used the village's meetinghouse for these examinations. The villagers squeezed onto the building's long wooden benches. Betty Parris, Betty Hubbard, Ann Putnam, and Abigail Williams sat in front.

Hathorne did the questioning, and he chose to speak to Sarah Good first. From the start, he didn't bother asking her if she was a witch. He already seemed to believe that she was. Instead, he asked her why and how she hurt the girls. Sarah explained that she was innocent. She said she had never practiced witchcraft against anyone.

not having committed a crime

Judge John Hathorne (seated at right) questions an accused witch (standing) as her accuser sits beside her.

As Good spoke, the four girls went into fits. They cried out that she was tormenting them right there in the meetinghouse. They said her spirit had left her body and was lunging toward them. Their disturbing behavior created an intense feeling of fear in the meetinghouse. It helped strengthen people's belief that the girls were truly bewitched.

Hathorne was also disturbed by what he saw. "Sarah Good," he said, "do you not see now what you have done [to the girls]? Why do you not tell us the truth?"

Once again, Good told him that she was innocent. But Hathorne did not believe her. He did not believe Sarah Osborne either when she tried to defend herself. He seemed to have decided beforehand that all three women were guilty. Yet the main evidence against them was the words and actions of the four girls.

having committed a crime

Hathorne questioned Tituba last. Unlike Good and Osborne, she chose to confess. She said she was guilty of being a witch. The devil had come to her, she said. He had forced her to hurt the four girls, and she was very sorry for it. She also said that Good and Osborne were witches. As soon as she confessed, the girls grew quiet and calm.

to admit to a crime

Tituba, Good, and Osborne were sent to prison. There they had to wait until they could be put on trial. The trial was supposed to determine if they were guilty or not. If they were found guilty, they would be hanged to death.

Tituba was questioned more in jail. She said that at least six other people were lurking about as witches. They lived in Salem

WHY DID TITUBA CONFESS?

After the Salem Witch Trials, Tituba said that Parris had beaten her into confessing. She probably also realized that she was better off telling Hathorne what he wanted to hear. That way she could promise to stop being a witch and help punish other witches. Her decision to confess saved her life. Of the three women, Tituba was the only one who survived the Salem Witch Trials.

This is the written record of Tituba's questioning on March 1, 1692.

and other communities, she said. Her words turned the villagers' growing fear into panic. Over the next days and weeks, they lived in terror. Children and adults had nightmares of witches harming them. They imagined seeing witches on dark paths and in shadows. They became suspicious of one another. Anyone could be a witch. No one was safe.

The girls began naming other villagers as witches. As soon as one witch was put in jail, they complained of another witch tormenting them. To make matters worse, several more girls from the village began to fall ill. They also accused witches of hurting them. In all, about eight girls made most of the accusations. At times, they seemed to work together. If one of them named a witch, the others chimed in to agree.

WHAT CAUSED THE GIRLS TO ACCUSE SO MANY PEOPLE?

Were the bewitched girls cruel troublemakers? Or did they truly believe they were bewitched? For years historians have tried to answer that question. Some have wondered if the girls suffered from actual illnesses. For example, a certain type of food poisoning can cause a person to see and feel things that aren't real. So can mental illnesses such as schizophrenia. It is also possible that adults encouraged the girls to make accusations against their enemies. Many historians believe the girls got caught up in the excitement of their lies. After the trials, one girl even admitted that she did it all for fun. Their behavior remains one of the great mysteries of the Salem Witch Trials.

Normally Puritan girls were under a lot of pressure to be silent and obedient. Their communities expected them to do as they were told without complaining. That meant spending hours doing chores such as sewing, cooking, and caring for younger children. It meant sitting in church for five hours each Sunday. It meant keeping their thoughts, feelings, and desires to themselves.

On top of that, many of these girls had very difficult lives. Some were orphans whose whole families had been violently killed in King William's War. Others were powerless servants with no one to care for them. When they claimed to be victims of witchcraft, suddenly their lives changed. Friends and neighbors prayed for them. Ministers came from other towns to see them. Everyone wanted to hear what they had to say. If they named someone as a witch, that person was usually questioned and sent to jail.

A girl accuses Captain John Alden Jr. of performing witchcraft in Salem.

At first the bewitched girls named unpopular villagers. But after a while, they seemed to test their power by accusing respected women in the community. These women were devoted Puritans. They had good reputations and came from well-liked families. They did not fit people's idea of a witch, yet they also ended up in jail waiting to be put on trial.

Although most villagers believed the girls, a small number began to doubt their stories. Some of these villagers spoke out about their doubts. The girls ended up accusing many of them of being witches too. After that, most people learned to keep their doubts to themselves.

NEXT QUESTION

WHEN DID THE FIRST WITCH TRIAL TAKE PLACE?

The townspeople of Salem accuse a woman of witchcraft. Within months of the first accusation, people all over the region were put in jail and faced witchcraft trials.

FOUR ON TRIAL

By late spring, dozens of women and men had been named as witches. The Salem Village girls had accused many of those people. But adults had also started to make accusations. In all, around sixty people accused witches of torturing them.

Only fifteen of the accused witches lived in Salem Village. The rest lived in surrounding towns. They were housewives, farmers, businessmen, craftspeople, military leaders, and ministers. Even some children had been accused and sent to jail. The youngest was Sarah Good's four-year-old daughter, Dorcas.

In May the colony's governor, Sir William Phips, set up a new court in Salem Town. One of the court's main jobs would be to oversee the trials of accused witches. Phips chose his deputy governor, William Stoughton, to be the court's chief judge. Stoughton had been a minister before becoming a political leader. The court's eight other judges had training as businessmen, doctors, and military leaders. None of them was trained in the law.

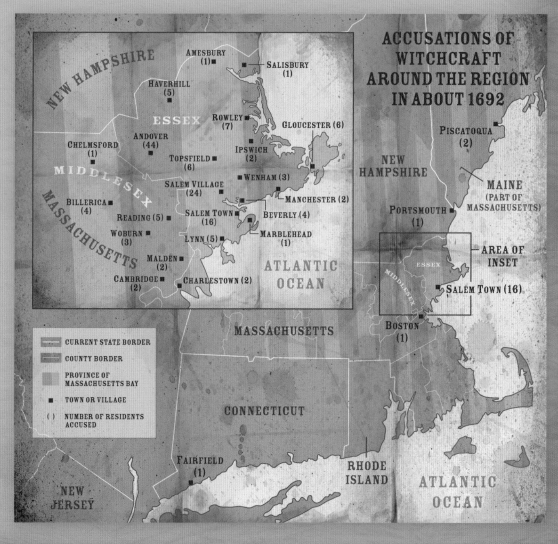

ACCUSATIONS OF WITCHCRAFT AROUND THE REGION IN ABOUT 1692

NEW HAMPSHIRE

AMESBURY (1)

SALISBURY (1)

HAVERHILL (5)

ESSEX

ROWLEY (7)

GLOUCESTER (6)

PISCATOQUA (2)

ANDOVER (44)

CHELMSFORD (1)

TOPSFIELD (6)

IPSWICH (2)

NEW HAMPSHIRE

MAINE (PART OF MASSACHUSETTS)

MIDDLESEX

WENHAM (3)

SALEM VILLAGE (24)

MANCHESTER (2)

BILLERICA (4)

READING (5)

SALEM TOWN (16)

BEVERLY (4)

PORTSMOUTH (1)

AREA OF INSET

WOBURN (3)

LYNN (5)

MARBLEHEAD (1)

MASSACHUSETTS

MALDEN (2)

ATLANTIC OCEAN

ESSEX

SALEM TOWN (16)

CAMBRIDGE (2)

CHARLESTOWN (2)

MIDDLESEX

CURRENT STATE BORDER

COUNTY BORDER

PROVINCE OF MASSACHUSETTS BAY

TOWN OR VILLAGE

( ) NUMBER OF RESIDENTS ACCUSED

MASSACHUSETTS

BOSTON (1)

CONNECTICUT

FAIRFIELD (1)

RHODE ISLAND

ATLANTIC OCEAN

NEW JERSEY

The job of the judges was to ask questions and run a fair trial. They did not have the power to decide if an accused witch was guilty or innocent. That job went to the court's jury. This group of twelve men was supposed to carefully consider all the evidence that came up during the trial. At the end of the trial, the jury would make its verdict.

twelve people from a community chosen to sit in judgment of an accused person during a trial. During the Salem Witch Trials, all jury members were men.

the final decision at the end of a trial, which states whether a person is believed to be guilty or not guilty

The first witch trial began on June 2, 1692. It was for an accused witch named Bridget Bishop. That day in court, the judges treated Bishop as if she were already guilty. So did many community members. They blamed her for causing illness and even death. Some neighbors said they had found witchcraft tools in her house years earlier.

The Salem Village girls were the most outspoken. They told stories of how Bishop flew out of her body to hurt them in their homes. They said

WHAT WAS LIFE LIKE FOR THE PRISONERS?

For the accused, life in the crowded prisons was often unbearable. Jailers chained them to walls in dark underground rooms. The chains were supposed to keep their spirits from flying out of their bodies and hurting people. The prisoners received little food or water. Even worse, they had to pay for their keep. Prisoners were charged for food, clothing, and bedding. They even had to pay for transportation to and from court. If they had no money, they got nothing at all. By the end of the trials, some families had used up their life's savings to care for a family member in jail.

she pinched, choked, and even tried to drown one of them. As they spoke, they often cried out in pain.

Again and again, Bishop said she was innocent. For the jury, it came down to her word against everyone else's. There was no other evidence against her. In the end, the jury found her guilty of being a witch.

Eight days later, Bishop was taken from prison to her hanging. She was probably brought to a rocky hill outside of Salem Town. It later became known as Witches Hill. Many people came to watch her die. The bewitched girls shouted at her and called her names. Everyone stared as Bishop was tied to an oak tree by her neck and hanged.

Bridget Bishop was found guilty of being a witch in 1692. Her punishment was death by hanging. She was the first person killed in the Salem Witch Trials.

HOW HAVE COURTS CHANGED SINCE THE WITCH TRIALS?

In modern U.S. courts, every accused person has the right to a fair trial. An important part of that right involves how judges and jury members treat the accused person. They must go into a trial thinking of the accused person as being innocent. An accused person should be found guilty only if enough real evidence proves his or her guilt. All accused people also have the right to a lawyer. Accused witches such as Bridget Bishop did not have these rights.

Although most people thought Bishop got what she deserved, some were upset by her death. One of those people was a judge in Stoughton's court. He did not think Bishop had gotten a fair trial. His concerns made no difference, so he quit.

A group of respected ministers wrote a letter to Governor Phips. They asked him to make sure

Massachusetts governor Sir William Phips (left) and his appointed chief judge, William Stoughton (right), were key figures in sending dozens of men and women to jail—or worse—during the Salem Witch Trials.

the court was run more fairly. They didn't think the bewitched girls' stories should be allowed as evidence. After all, the girls could be confused or even lying. Perhaps the devil had tricked them into naming all these witches. The ministers' concerns fell on deaf ears.

The next trial took place on June 29. That morning a woman named Rebecca Nurse came before the court. Nurse had been a respected member of Salem Village. She had always been a good Puritan and neighbor. Unlike Bishop, many people came to her defense. Thirty-nine people had signed a petition on her behalf. In this document, they argued that Nurse was innocent. They begged for her to be set free. They wrote, "We never had any cause or grounds to suspect her of any such thing as she is now accused."

Thirty-nine people signed this petition in 1692 declaring that Rebecca Nurse could not be a witch.

At the trial, Nurse's accusers claimed that she had caused them great suffering. The girls went into fits and cried out in court. But the jury also heard from people who sided with Nurse. At the end of the trial, the twelve men reached their verdict. They said that Nurse was not guilty. That meant she could go free.

This decision sent a powerful message to the community. It said that the bewitched girls had been wrong about Nurse. And if they were wrong about Nurse, they might be wrong about other people. This idea had the power to keep the witch trials from getting out of control.

Then Judge Stoughton stepped in.

An illustration by Howard Pyle shows court officials questioning Rebecca Nurse during her trial. The jury found her not guilty before Judge Stoughton encouraged it to change its verdict.

Nurse is led in chains through the meetinghouse where the church pastor excommunicated her (officially excluded her as a member of the church).

He asked the jury to rethink its decision. He made it clear that he disagreed with it. Judges were not supposed to tell a jury what to think. Judges were only supposed to help the jury understand the evidence. But the jury respected the chief judge. They changed their minds and found Nurse guilty. On July 19, she and four other women were hanged to death.

NEXT QUESTION

HOW MANY PEOPLE WERE PUT TO DEATH DURING THE WITCH TRIALS?

Howard Pyle illustrated this scene of two accused witches entering the courtroom. Their accusers (seated) point at them in fear and go into fits.

FIVE SO THAT NO MORE INNOCENT BLOOD BE SHED

Several more trials took place over the summer. For the accused, they must have been terrifying experiences. Everyone was against them—the judges, the community, and the jury. And the bewitched girls added to the tension in the courtroom. Usually they went into fits as soon as an accused person entered the courtroom.

During the trials, the girls often acted as if they were being controlled like puppets. If an accused witch squeezed her hands in court, the girls screamed that she was pinching them. If she bit her lips, the girls said she was biting them. If she tilted her head, the girls cried out that she was breaking their necks.

Each trial ended the same way—with a guilty verdict. Out of desperation, some people decided to confess after their trial. Oddly, confessing was the one way to avoid being hanged. Confessing was also how prisoners avoided going to trial. People who confessed promised to stop performing witchcraft. They also agreed to help local officials by naming other witches. Often their words were used as evidence. In all, more than fifty people gave confessions.

In this engraving, Salem officials visit an accused witch in jail to convince her to write a confession. Confessing would spare her life.

Other accused people wrote petitions. In these letters, the accused argued for their innocence and pleaded for their freedom. One woman wrote an especially powerful petition. Her name was Mary Easty. Easty had already been put on trial and found guilty. Before her hanging, she sent a passionate letter to the judges.

Easty wrote, "I petition your honours not for my own life, for I know I must die, and my appointed time is set." Instead, she was writing so that "no more innocent blood be shed."

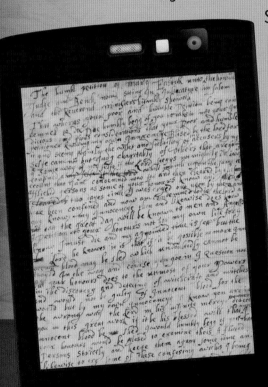

She insisted that the girls were lying, and she begged the judges not to believe everything they said. Although her words were strong and heartfelt, they didn't change the judges' minds.

By the end of September 1692, Easty was one of nineteen people who had been hanged. Fourteen of them were

Mary Easty, a sister of Rebecca Nurse, was sentenced to death in her trial. Easty wrote a petition to the judge and jury to stop the punishment of innocent people.

This stone bench is part of a memorial wall in Salem. Giles Corey, an accused witch, died under the weight of heavy stones laid on his body to torture him into confessing.

women, and five were men. Another man had been crushed to death for refusing to be put on trial. And the judges weren't anywhere close to being done. They continued to prepare for more trials.

These deadly facts didn't change the behavior of the bewitched girls. They and other villagers continued to name more people as witches. At least 160 people were accused. Most of them waited in overflowing jails for their trial.

Certain leaders in Massachusetts were growing alarmed. They worried that a dangerous fear of witches might take over the entire colony. They also questioned the way the witch trials were being run. They feared that innocent people had been put to death.

One of those leaders was Increase Mather. Mather was the most powerful and respected minister in the colony. He was also known as a wise political leader. In October he spoke out against the trials. "It were better that ten suspected witches should escape," he wrote, "than that one innocent person should be condemned [sentenced to death]." His words echoed the thoughts of a growing number of people in the colony.

On October 12, Governor Phips decided to shut down the court. He created a new one

Increase Mather helped end the killing of accused witches in Salem. U.S. artist John van der Spriett painted this portrait of Mather in 1688.

that would follow much stricter rules. From then on, the stories
of the bewitched girls
and other accusers
would no longer count
as evidence against
someone. The court
had to uncover other
evidence to prove
beyond doubt that an accused person had practiced harmful
witchcraft.

> "It were better that ten suspected witches should escape than that one innocent person should be condemned."
> —Increase Mather

Phips opened the new court in January 1693. That winter fifty-two more people were put on trial. Under the court's new rules, nearly everyone on trial was found not guilty. The jury found only three people guilty. Governor Phips ended up freeing those people as well. By May he had also freed more than one hundred people still waiting in prison.

The Salem Witch Trials had finally come to an end, but the pain they caused did not go away. At least twenty-four people were dead, including four who had died in prison. The families of these men and women had suffered terribly. The rest of the village also suffered. They had turned against one another. Somehow they had to find a way to forgive one another and learn from the past.

NEXT QUESTION

WHY DID SAMUEL PARRIS LEAVE SALEM?

No one executed in the Salem Witch Trials was buried in the village cemetery. A memorial wall, later built beside the Old Burying Point Cemetery, contains twenty-seven benches bearing the names of the wrongly accused.

SIX AFTER THE TRIALS

For three years, the people responsible for the Salem Witch Trials remained silent. They made no apologies and admitted to no wrongdoing. It wasn't until 1697 that the colony began to acknowledge the painful past.

On January 14, the people of Massachusetts observed a day of remembrance. They prayed and fasted (went without food). They remembered the people who had suffered because of the Salem Witch Trials. A judge from the Salem court apologized for his part in those painful events. His name was Samuel Sewall. The jury members also signed an apology. In it they wrote, "We do heartily ask forgiveness of you all." None of the other judges apologized.

Samuel Parris also remained silent. But many villagers believed their minister owed them an apology. They felt he had flamed the fires of fear with his sermons. He had done nothing to stop the accusations or the trials. In fact, many people believed he had encouraged them. After the trials, the village turned against him. In 1697 he left Salem for good.

It took nine more years for one of the eight young accusers to make a public apology. At the age of twenty-nine, Ann Putnam wrote, "[I] earnestly beg forgiveness of God and from all those unto whom I have given just cause of sorrow and offense, whose relations were taken away or accused."

Nathaniel Emmons painted this portrait of Judge Samuel Sewall in 1728. Sewall was the only witch trials judge who admitted any wrongdoing.

The Salem Witchcraft Victims' Memorial at Danvers, Massachusetts, was dedicated to the victims of the Salem Witchcraft Trials in 1992, three hundred years after their deaths.

She had come to believe that the devil had "deluded," or misled, her at the time. The past must have weighed heavily on her for she wrote, "I desire to lie in the dust, and be humbled for it." She was the only member of the group of bewitched girls to ever apologize.

In 1711 the colony of Massachusetts finally started to make amends for the Salem Witch Trials. It began to offer money to

"[I] earnestly beg forgiveness of God and from all those unto whom I have given just cause of sorrow and offense."

—Ann Putnam

the families of those who had been hanged. It also began to change the verdicts of the trials from guilty to not guilty. Leaders hoped to restore the reputations of the accused. But it was not until 1957 that Massachusetts officially apologized for the Salem Witch Trials.

The story of Salem reminds us of what can happen when a community acts out of fear and resentment. It also reminds us of the dangers of an unfair court system. The right to a fair trial has become one of our nation's most strongly held values. More than three hundred years have passed since the Salem Witch Trials. Yet it remains an important story in American History.

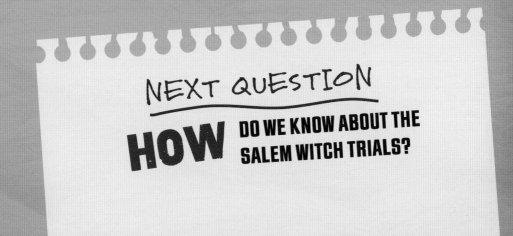

NEXT QUESTION

HOW DO WE KNOW ABOUT THE SALEM WITCH TRIALS?

Primary Source: Ann Putnam's Declaration against Mary Easty

We know about the Salem Witch Trials from writings of the time. Official documents recorded who was accused of being a witch and who made the accusations. Records were also kept of what happened during examinations and trials. In addition, other people wrote books and letters about the events surrounding the witch trials. All of these papers are important primary sources.

A primary source is a document written by a person who was alive at the time of an event. It is often a firsthand description of something that happened in history. Letters, journals, and newspaper articles are examples of primary sources. The primary source below was used at Mary Easty's trial as evidence that she was a witch. It came from the young Ann Putnam.

> Mary Easty did most grievously torment me during the time of her examination. Also on the same day I saw Mary Easty or her appearance [spirit] most grievously torment and afflict Mary Walcott, Mercy Lewes, Elizabeth Hubbard, and Abigail Williams and I verily believe in my heart that Mary Easty is a most dreadful witch and that she hath very often afflicted me and the persons afore named by her acts of witchcraft.
>
> Ann Putnam: declared: to the Jury of Inquest: that her above written evidence: is the truth upon her oath: August 4: 1692.

TELL YOUR SALEM WITCHCRAFT TRIALS STORY

Imagine that you are a reporter at one of the witch trials. You have to write an article about what happens. You'll need to include all the important facts about the event. For example:

WHEN did the trial take place?

WHERE was the trial held?

WHAT was the name of the accused person?

WHY was he or she accused of witchcraft?

WHO else was at the trial?

HOW did the jury make its decision?

USE **WHO, WHAT, WHERE WHY, WHEN,** AND **HOW** TO THINK OF OTHER QUESTIONS TO HELP YOU CREATE YOUR STORY!

Timeline

1689

Native American fighters attack a town in New Hampshire in June, starting what became known as King William's War.

Samuel Parris becomes Salem Village's new minister in November.

1692

Betty Parris and Abigail Williams come down with a strange illness in January. A doctor eventually concludes they are bewitched.

On February 25, Parris's slaves, Tituba and John, agree to make a witch cake. The next day, Betty and Abigail claim that **Tituba** is a witch who has been tormenting them. Two other girls accuse Sarah Good and Sarah Osborne of being witches.

John Hathorne and Jonathan Corwin arrive on March 1 to question Tituba, Sarah Good, and Sarah Osborne. Tituba confesses to being a witch.

In the spring, more girls claim they are bewitched. They accuse others of being witches. Some adults also make accusations.

Sir William Phips creates a court in Salem Town to handle the witch trials. William Stoughton is the court's chief judge.

Bridget Bishop is the first accused person to stand trial on June 2. The jury finds her guilty. Bishop is hanged eight days later.

Twelve ministers of the colony write a letter protesting the way Bishop's trial was handled.

On June 29, five more accused witches stand trial. They include Sarah Good and Rebecca Nurse. The jury finds all the women guilty except Nurse. But the jurors change their decision about Nurse after Stoughton asks them to reconsider it. On July 19, 1692, all five are hanged.

Twenty-one people are put on trial for witchcraft in August and September. All are found guilty. Thirteen are hanged.

In October, Increase Mather speaks out against the witch trials. Governor Phips shuts down the court in Salem Town.

1693

Governor Phips opens a new court in January with stricter rules about running fair trials. In these trials, only three out of fifty-two people are found guilty. No one is put to death.

Governor Phips ends the witch trials by freeing more than one hundred accused persons still in jail in May.

1697

On January 14, the colony sets aside a day to remember the tragedy of the Salem Witch Trials. **Judge Samuel Sewall** makes a public apology. The jury also signs a written apology.

Samuel Parris leaves Salem Village that fall.

1706

Ann Putnam publicly apologizes for her part in the Salem Witch Trials.

1711

The colony of Massachusetts declares most of the people hanged innocent, and it begins to pay money to their families.

1752

Salem Village officially separates from Salem Town. Five years later, it becomes the town of Danvers.

1957

The State of Massachusetts officially apologizes for the Salem Witch Trials.

1972

The Salem Witch Museum opens in Salem, Massachusetts.

Source Notes

20 Marilynne K. Roach, *The Salem Witch Trials: A Day-by-Day Chronicle of a Community Under Siege* (New York: Cooper Square Press, 2002), 26.

29 Frances Hill, *A Delusion of Satan: The Full Story of the Salem Witch Trials* (Cambridge, MA: Da Capo Press, 2002), 156.

34 Paul Boyer and Stephen Nissenbaum, *Salem Possessed* (Cambridge, MA: Harvard University Press, 1974), 8.

36 Boyer and Nissenbaum, *Salem Possessed*, 10.

37 Ibid.

39 Hill, *A Delusion of Satan*, 207.

39 Ibid.

40 Roach, *Salem Witch Trials*, 569.

40 Ibid.

41–42 Ibid.

42 "Ann Putnam, Jr. v. Mary Easty," in *The Salem Witchcraft Papers, Volume 1: Verbatim Transcripts of the Legal Documents of the Salem Witchcraft Outbreak of 1692*, eds. Paul Boyer and Stephen Nissenbaum (New York: Da Capo Press, 1977), available online at http://etext.virginia.edu/etcbin/toccer-new2?id=BoySal1.sgm&images=images/modeng&data=/texts/english/modeng/oldsalem&tag=public&part=254&division=div2 (December 2009).

Bibliography

Boyer, Paul, and Stephen Nissenbaum. *Salem Possessed*. Cambridge, MA: Harvard University Press, 1974.

———, eds. *The Salem Witchcraft Papers, Volumes 1–3: Verbatim Transcripts of the Legal Documents of the Salem Witchcraft Outbreak of 1692*. New York: Da Capo Press, 1977. Available online at http://etext.virginia.edu/salem/witchcraft/texts/transcripts.html (August 24, 2011).

Delbanco, Andrew. *The Puritan Ordeal*. Cambridge, MA: Harvard University Press, 1989.

Francis, Richard. *Judge Sewell's Apology: The Salem Witch Trials and the Forming of an American Conscience*. New York: Fourth Estate, 2005.

Hill, Frances. *A Delusion of Satan: The Full Story of the Salem Witch Trials*. Cambridge, MA: Da Capo Press, 2002.

Hoffer, Peter. *The Devil's Disciples: Makers of the Salem Witchcraft Trials*. Baltimore: Johns Hopkins University Press, 1996.

Karlsen, Carol F. *The Devil in the Shape of a Woman: Witchcraft in Colonial New England*. New York: Norton, 1987.

LaPlante, Eve. *Salem Witch Judge: The Life and Repentance of Samuel Sewall*. New York: HarperOne, 2007.

Norton, Mary Beth. *In the Devil's Snare: The Salem Witchcraft Crisis of 1692*. New York: Alfred A. Knopf, 2002.

Roach, Marilynne K. *The Salem Witch Trials: A Day-by-Day Chronicle of a Community Under Siege*. New York: Cooper Square Press, 2002.

Ziff, Larzer. *Puritanism in America: A New Culture in a New World*. New York: Viking Press, 1973.

Further Reading and Websites

Kerns, Ann. *Wizards and Witches*. Minneapolis: Lerner Publications Company, 2010. Explore the creepy tales and mystical stories of these magical beings that have fascinated people since ancient times.

Knudsen, Shannon. *Alice Ray and the Salem Witch Trials*. Minneapolis: Millbrook Press, 2011. In this story, a friend of Ann Putnam struggles with what to do when people she feels are innocent have been accused of witchcraft. The book includes a reader's theater play.

Miller, William. *Tituba*. San Diego: Gulliver Books, 2000. This biography uncovers the life of the first woman accused during the Salem Witch Trials.

Puritans—History for Kids
http://www.historyforkids.org/learn/northamerica/after1500/religion/puritans.htm
Visit this Web page to learn more about the Puritans and their history.

Salem Witch Museum
http://www.salemwitchmuseum.com/
This official website includes information about the events of 1692.

The Salem Witch Trials—*National Geographic Kids*
http://kids.nationalgeographic.com/Stories/History/Salem-witch-trials
This Web page offers information and photos about Salem during the time of the witch trials.

Yolen, Jane, and Heidi Elisabet Yolen Stemple. *The Salem Witch Trials: An Unsolved Mystery from History*. New York: Simon & Schuster, 2004. The authors help readers to think like detectives to understand why the fear of witches took over the village of Salem.

Index

Photo Acknowledgments

The images in this book are used with the permission of: © iStockphoto.com/DNY59, p. 1; © Keng Po Leung/Dreamstime.com, p. 1 (background) and all rope backgrounds; © iStockphoto.com/sx70, pp. 3 (top), 9 (top), 14, 15 (top), 21 (left), 22, 26, 28 (top), 36 (top), 41; © iStockphoto.com/Ayse Nazli Deliormanli, pp. 3 (bottom), 43 (left); © iStockphoto.com/Serdar Yagci, pp. 4–5 (background), 43 (background); © Bill Hauser and Laura Westlund/Independent Picture Service, pp. 4–5 (map); © iStockphoto.com/Andrey Pustovoy, pp. 4, 29, 34; © Erin Paul Donovan/SuperStock, p. 4 (inset); © North Wind Picture Archives, pp. 5, 6, 19, 21 (right), 23 (top); © iStockphoto.com/Talshiar, p. 7; © Laura Westlund/Independent Picture Service, pp. 7 (inset), 25; © Wikimedia Foundation , Inc., p. 8; © Massachusetts Historical Society, Boston, MA, USA/The Bridgeman Art Library, pp. 9 (bottom), 36 (bottom), 39, 45; The Granger Collection, New York, pp. 10, 13, 15 (bottom), 16, 17 (top), 18, 33, 44; Cornell University Library, Making of America Digital Collection, p. 12; © Baldwin H. Ward & Kathryn C. Ward/CORBIS, p. 24; © George Eastman House/Archive Photos/Getty Images, p. 27; Courtesy of the Maine State Museum, p. 28 (bottom left); © Old Paper Studios/Alamy, p. 28 (bottom right); Courtesy of the Massachusetts Historical Society, p. 29 (inset); © Everett Collection/SuperStock, pp. 30, 31 (top); © Bettmann/CORBIS, p. 32; Essex County Archives, Salem, Massachusetts, Photograph courtesy of the Peabody Essex Museum, p. 34 (inset); © Nancy Carter/North Wind Picture Archives, p. 35; © Maurice Savage/Alamy, p. 38; © Lee Snider/Photo Images/CORBIS, p. 40; © Peabody Essex Museum, Salem, Massachusetts/The Bridgeman Art Library/Getty Images, p. 43 (right).

Front cover: © Peabody Essex Museum, Salem, Massachusetts/The Bridgeman Art Library/Getty Images. Back cover: © Keng Po Leung/Dreamstime.com (background).

Main body text set in Sassoon Sans Regular 13.5/20. Typeface provided by Monotype Typography.